SurrendertoSuffer

YoVanda-Ray A. Jenkins

SurrendertoSuffer

To Live In Christ Is Gain

A Division of WINEPRESS PUBLISHING

ISBN 13: 978-1-4141-0920-6
ISBN 10: 1-4141-0920-2
Library of Congress Catalog Card Number: 2006910614

Dedication

This Book is dedicated to:
My Grandmothers, Esther Hackett and Gertrude Brown, who have gone on home to be with the Lord. They were very special and important women in my life.

A very dear and unique friend, Evangelist Sheila Bridges, who has also gone home to be with the Lord.

I thank God for placing these godly, virtuous women in my life. They have deposited a wealth of godly instructions into me and I thank God for their being women who availed themselves of the His spirit. My grandmother Esther and Evangelist Sheila departed this life in 1999, one in March and the other in October. My grandmother Gertrude departed this life in August 2005. They are part of the reason I am able to share this book with you today.

I also dedicate this book to Evangelist Sarah Jackson. She was the one God used to speak life to the seed that was within me to write this book during the summer of 1992.

Table of Contents

Foreword

It is very evident that we must suffer with Christ if we are to reign with Him. Pastor Vanda Jenkins has made me more aware than ever before that suffering is a part of salvation–no pain, no gain.

We don't understand why bad things happen to good people, but we know that all things work for our good if we love the Lord and are called according to His purpose. This author has conveyed and has executed this point very well, even to the point of undressing herself naked for all to see. As I read, I might have been knocked down a few times, but yet I rise through the power of a forgiving and repentant heart.

The word "surrender" simply means to submit, to give one's will to another. Pastor Vanda has in my opinion, totally surrendered to the power of God and also to the author inside of her.

Daughter, I commend you for exposing your wounds to your readers, an audience of your peers, to help someone who is suffering, but yet doesn't know how to surrender.

This book will cause you to look inside of yourself and know that if you surrender to God, your suffering will bring victory—if you stay on the wheel.

I am honored to have been chosen to write the foreword for this masterpiece.

Apostle William G. Smack, Sr., Agape Ministries, Inc., Seaford, DE 19973.

Acknowledgements

To my husband, William (Billy), my daughters, Nikeah and Kierra and my sons, Tyrell and Trevon–thank you for sharing me with so many people that God has sent my way to support, encourage and minister a word of life too. I also thank you for allowing me to have this time to be able to write this book. I want you all to know how much I appreciate and love you for encouraging me and supporting me.

To my parents–Veronica, my mother, thank you for giving me life. Raymond, thank you for loving me as your very own and showing me life. David, thank you for being the seed that God used to give me life.

Most of all, to my Heavenly Father, the creator of my life—thank you for my trials and tribulations because they came to make me strong. Thank you for my joyous times because I realize they came between the storms to encourage me to hold on.

Introduction

This book is to anyone who has ever had to struggle with any type of issue, circumstance, or problem. *Surrender to Suffer* was designed to show you that your issues, be they great or small, were fashioned to fit you and to make you grow. Your trials and tribulations didn't come your way for no reason at all. God has a purpose and a plan in mind for sending them your way, so learn from them. It is up to you how you perceive your problems. God wants to share His dreams and thoughts with you no matter what you have been through. If you allow Him, God is able to see you through all past hurts, torn emotions, rejections, times of being misunderstood, and periods of loneliness. He wants you to cast your cares on Him because He cares for you. Don't hold onto your pain of the past; release it and let it go. God has greater things for you than the memories of your father or mother not being in your life, being on drugs, some man or woman walking out on you and leaving you with the kids, having your car repossessed, or getting fired, raped, molested, or abused. Whatever it is, LET IT GO. God wants to heal you and make you whole and complete.

My prayer as you read this book is that you will realize God is speaking to you about your situations and how He wants to resolve them. Let Him speak to your heart to show you how to love. Let Him speak in your ears to show you that you can listen. Let Him look into your eyes to show you that you can see through His eyes, and let Him touch you to show you that He is real. I also pray that He reveals Himself and His will to you, so the next time you go through suffering, you will allow His Holy Spirit to lead and guide you to grow through it as well.

While reading this book, my brother or sister, allow the words to be a prescription to heal you from what you have gone through, what you are going through, or what you will go through. We have to grasp that to live in Christ is gain.

Chapter 1

Do I Really
Have to Suffer?

Be sober, be vigilant; because your adversary the Devil, as a
roaring lion, walketh about, seeking whom he may devour:
Whom resist steadfast in the faith, knowing that the same
afflictions are accomplished in your brethren that are in the
world. But the God of all grace, who hath called us unto his
eternal glory by Christ Jesus, after that ye have suffered a
while, make you perfect, stablish, strengthen, settle you.

—1 Peter 5:8-10 (KJV)

It is necessary that we suffer because our adversary the Devil
is walking around seeking whom he may devour. To devour
means to consume. The Devil wants to destroy us, totally consume us. He has a contract out on our lives because he knows
once we get over our past and get rid of our fears, we are going
to tear his kingdom down. The battle is on and will continue to
be on between the Devil and God until the second coming of
Christ. It is up to us to be sober, which means we have a sound

mind and maintain self-control. It is very important that we be vigilant, ever watchful. After all, the Bible tells us to watch as well as pray. (See Mark 13:33 and Luke 21:36)

In order to understand our adversary as a roaring lion, we need to know some facts about a lion. Usually lions hunt at night when the dim light helps to keep them hidden from their prey. Lions have a good night vision so the darkness doesn't pose a problem for them. Also, mostly the female lions do the hunting. Lions might spend hours-stalking prey but the actual kill is made in just minutes. After the kill is made, the female lets out low roars. This tells the pride to join the meal. Adult males eat first, followed by females and then the cubs. However, the male lion's roar can be heard up to 5 miles away.

This tells us that Devil keeps himself hidden from us during our dark seasons, while he is stalking us to make his move on an attempt to kill (devour) us. This may be why it appears that we are hit with one thing after another because the males come in to eat, the females come, and then the cubs. It's like the bites of life don't stop and we may mentality become lethargic.

If our thinking is not clear and we are not watchful, how will we be able to recognize the Devil as a roaring lion? You see, the Devil's roaring-lion disguise to you may be an abusive relationship. He might show up as drugs or alcohol. An illicit sexual relationship might be his ruse. Or he might roar up to you as greed, witchcraft, pride, jealousy, envy, malice, lying, killing, stealing, cheating, or any such thing.

I remember when Satan "roared" at me after I gave birth to my daughter, Kierra. During the pregnancy, I had developed toxemia and delivered her during the seventh month. The "roar" had convinced me, that it was my fault, that we both almost died and that she was premature because I had stressed myself to near death (the reason why is in another chapter). I believed that lie for a day or two and didn't go to the Neonatal Care Unit to visit my baby. The "roar" was so loud (it seemed like it was heard 5 miles away) that I was too frightened to face the gift that God had given me due to the guilt within. However, I did get enough courage and strength to go visit my baby. Even though, her little body had tubes everywhere, I had to speak back to the Devil and tell him that he is a liar, "My baby shall live." She had minor birth defects. She is a senior in high school a will graduate this year 2007.

Sometimes we get so caught up in the pain of our present or our past that we are not able to focus on Christ. Our issues are so real and vivid that we do not realize there is a reason for our suffering. God knows the reason and He wants to share it with us, but we are so consumed with the weights of those issues that we don't take the time to fall on our faces before the All Sufficient One to find out what is going on. Instead of listening, we dissolve into panic and start asking, "Why is this happening to me?" or, "I can't take no more," and "Why me, Lord?"

In actuality, what we should be saying is, "Why not me?" If we stop long enough to appreciate what Christ went through for us, we would not have so many personal pity parties.

Isaiah 53 tells us what Jesus went through for us. It says that He was despised and rejected by men, He was a man of sorrows and well acquainted with grief. He carried our griefs and sorrows. He was wounded by reason of our transgressions. In other words, His skin was torn, pierced, and cut because we violated the law or command. We were the ones who sinned, not He. He was bruised for our iniquities. Because of our iniquities (wickedness),

He was brusied and that means the soft tissue of His body had been injured. Small veins and capillaries (the tiniest blood vessels) under the skin sometimes break. Red blood cells leak out these blood vessels. The red blood cells that collect under the skin cause discoloration. The Scripture said He had no form of comeliness; and when we shall see him, there is no beauty that we should desire him.

Can you visualize what Jesus went through for us? He was oppressed and afflicted. And check this out; He didn't even open his mouth. How many times have we gone through situations and God has said to us, "Hush, I have everything under control," and we still open our big mouths and say something that we have no business saying? Then we wonder *Why do I have to suffer?*

We suffer for several reasons, but I believe the number one reason we suffer is because we can't keep our mouths closed so we can let Christ shine through us no matter what we're going through. We must realize that Jesus Christ suffered for us, and if we want to reign with Him, we must suffer too. It is not a weakness to keep our mouths closed when God tells us to be quiet. If we would close our mouths, our eyes would be much more attentive and we would be focused on watching Him work on our behalf. Many times when we go through our situations, we open our mouths and all sorts of negative words flow out.

The time has come for our tongues to be delivered. When God tells us to be quiet, it is for our good. Keeping our thoughts and comments to ourselves will require us to discipline our tongues. It is rude and out of order to speak when you have been asked to be quiet. We need to allow God to purge us, so we can do what He is expecting us to do. We are operating out of strength, not weakness, when we refrain from letting corrupt communication flow out of our mouths.

How respectful is your tongue towards God? Are you able to maintain your tongue and keep it still? Are you willing to put your emotions under the Blood of Jesus and allow Him to help you to restrain from venting when you are hurt, disappointed, and/or angry?

I remember an **outcome** of a conversation that I had with Cathy. I don't remember what we were talking about. But I do remember God tell me not to share my thought. However, we were girls, and I thought I could share anything. Well, of course the conversation didn't end on a pleasant note because **"I"** wasn't obedient to God. So I had to go back to her and apologize because I had been given divine orders to "Hush."

Remember the Bible passage that opened this chapter? I Peter 5:10 says, "But the God of all grace, who hath called us unto his eternal glory by Christ Jesus, after that ye have suffered a while, make you perfect, stablish, strengthen, settle you." (KJV) The Bible does not tell us the time span of "a while." All we're told is that being made perfect (mature), being established, and being strengthened and settled happens after we have suffered a while. We must trust God and wait on Him to end the "a while" of the suffering He's allowed. Our ways are not His ways, so our "a while" is not His "a while." We simply must trust that after we suffer a while, something is going to happen for our good in the plan of God.

I can recall when my daughter, Nikki who is 22 years old, was 8 years old and she was longing for her father, Kent, to be in her life. He was either still in the military or living in another state at the time. She would cry , fall on the floor and her little body would be shaking as if she were having convulsions. I would talk to her and let her know that I was here for her but nothing I said or did could stop the hurt inside of her. On Mother's Day that year, we were riding home from church and she was looking out the window with tears rolling down her face. I asked her what was wrong. She said, "I want my daddy." (I wanted to tell her girl, it is Mother's Day and I am the one that is with you and you are sitting here crying over him). However, I didn't express my feelings, but I did tell her that I don't know when or how God will work this out for you but if you just tell Him how you are hurting, He will hear your cry and answer your prayer. (I just wanted my child's "a while" to end and I knew my own words were not resolving her problem). So she prayed and expressed her pain to God, and almost one year later, God answered her prayer and her father moved back to his hometown, Hebron, with his parents and she was able to see her father.

Unfortunately, the majority of the time, we don't understand what God is doing with us, for us, and through us during our season of suffering. All we know is that we want the hurting to stop and we want it to stop now! Our tolerance level for enduring hardship like a good soldier is not very high. We do not enjoy suffering, so the human side of us wants it to end quickly. That's why we must trust our times, good and bad, to His hands.

As God's children, we need to learn to act like children and accept what He allows to come our way. Instead, we open our mouths and charge Him, others, and ourselves foolishly because we don't like what we're going through. We will only grow through what we go through. Our suffering will never amount to anything more than heartache and pain if we do not learn the lesson of the particular situation we currently face. There is an anointing fashioned to fit us for every trial that comes our way. In order for us to have success, we must have failure. To obtain success in our marriages, careers, singleness, and ministries, we must endure suffering.

Another reason why we suffer is because we don't have faith in God like we are supposed to. If God told you, "I'm going to allow you to go through a storm but no harm shall befall you," would you be able to have faith that indeed no harm would come upon you?

Let's say God allowed a venomous beast to bite you while your buddies were standing around watching. They would probably start panicking about the viper hanging from your hand.

"Man, you're getting ready to die because that snake is poisonous. It's been real, Brother, but we've got to go."

Your buddies don't stay around to help you, nor do they have a prayer meeting. They run because fear has set in and they are gone. They say to you, "See ya, we're out of here, peace out."

Would you get discouraged because your so-called buddies or pew partners left you all alone to die, or would you stand on the word God told you, that no harm would befall you? Would you even tell your friends what God told you so they could see God work?

When you are presented with situations that test your faith, how well does your faith come out? In Acts 28, Paul had a similar situation. I encourage you to read it and follow the example of Paul so your friends won't run away and leave you for dead. By believing God, you can allow your faith to be proven so your friends' minds can be changed. Your friends will be able to experience your God. Let's read Acts 28:1-6.

And when they were escaped, then they knew that the island was called Melita. And the barbarous People shewed us no little kindness: for they kindled a fire, and received us every one, because of the present rain, and because of the cold. And when the barbarians saw the venomous beast hang on his hand, they said among themselves, No doubt this man is a murderer, whom, though he hath escaped the sea, yet vengeance sufferth not to live. And he shook off the beast into the fire, and felt no harm. Howbeit they looked when he should have swollen, or fallen down dead suddenly: but after they had looked a great while, and saw no harm come to him, they changed their minds, and said that he was a god.

When we fail to obey God, we also suffer because we have people watching us and depending on us to make it through our tests, trials, and tribulations. They are cheering us on in their minds thinking, *If she can make it, I know that I can make it,* or they say to themselves, *If she made it through that, then I can make it through this.*

Let the life you live for God speak for you. Don't be worried about the opinions of other people. If you are bound by the opinions of others, receive your deliverance from the spirit of intimidation. 1 Peter 3:13 states, "and who is he that will harm you, if you be followers of that which is good?" You see, we have to know that in spite of what other people think of us or about us, we will be fine if we are doing what God tells us to do. We don't have to walk around afraid because people are watching us. Honey, whether we do good or bad, somebody will always be watching, looking, and peeping at us.

I remember during the first year of two of our marriage, that I got extremely upset and I shared with my friend, Sheila, that I was tired, fed up and I couldn't handle this marriage stuff anymore. She told me if I give up then I am putting my husband on a silver platter and telling Satan to do what you want with my husband because I don't believe God anymore. She then added that I would be hindering my witness of Christ because I am a woman of great faith. She said, "You never know who is watching your walk in Christ." I didn't want to hear what she was saying. I want my friend to talk to me, not the Evangelist. However, at that same time, she was going through problems in her marriage and she told me that she was encouraged by my faith to stay committed to her own marriage. I almost failed in my witness of Christ because I wasn't aware that she was watching the Christ in me so closely. She is deceased and I can't pick up the phone to call her anymore, but I'm thankful for the words she spoke to me. Her words made me to be more conscientious of my actions because I didn't know who would be or was watching me.

Do I really have to suffer? The answer is yes. We must go through our trials and tests in order to be able to participate in the fellowship of Christ's suffering. We must not complain while we are suffering. Our faith is being put to the test. We need patience in order for us to allow God's will to be done in our lives. My former Assistant Pastor, Rev. Dr. Keith Wongus, say many times that patience means to abide under pressure cheerfully. Understand the concept of patience. James 1:3-4 says, "Knowing this that the trying of your faith worketh patience. But let patience have her perfect work, that ye may be perfect and entire, wanting nothing." While employing our faith in order to grow, mature, and live a worry-free lifestyle in Jesus Christ, suffering causes us to abide under pressure cheerfully.

Chapter 2

Does Suffering Cause Me to Mature in the Lord?

Suffering will cause you to mature in the Lord when you do two things. First, line up your suffering with God's word; and second, line your life up with God's word while you are experiencing suffering and as you look back on suffering. Let's deal with each of these separately.

First, in order to allow suffering to mature you, you must line up your suffering with God's word. In other words, change how you perceive suffering. Suffering will cause you to mature in the Lord when you change how you perceive suffering. Look at I Peter 5:10 again. It says, "But the God of all grace, who hath called us unto his eternal glory by Christ Jesus, after that ye have suffered a while, make you perfect, stablish, strengthen, settle you." (KJV) Perfect means mature. Mature means to be able to go through situations and come out disciplined. To be disciplined means you allow your situation to teach you, producing Godly characteristics that will flourish out of your life. That nasty, ugly, and/or painful situation that is trying to destroy you can actually help to prosper you.

Now it doesn't matter how you entered into the situation-whether you walked into it, were thrown into it, or were pulled and pushed through it—the key to maturity is the knowledge and training you obtained from it that caused you to come out of the situation self-controlled and obedient to God. Sufferings, be they self-inflicted or caused of others, can be allowed to produce a level of maturity. They can take you from faith to faith and from glory to glory. However, if you fail to learn your lesson from your particular trial, you will see that trial again until you learn what God intended for you to learn.

Lets look at the 1st and 2nd Adam. The 1st Adam disobeyed God when he ate from the tree of knowledge of good and evil. God told him thou shalt not eat of it: for in the day that thou eatest thereof thou shalt surely die. Now it took 42 generations in order for God to get the obedience He desired man to obtain. That's why Jesus (2nd Adam) said, I came to save "that" which was lost (Matthew 18:11). The 2nd Adam had to be obedient unto to death which was swallowed up in victory because the 1st Adam's disobedience was the origin of death. It was sown in corruption; it was raised in incorruption. It was sown in dishonor; it is raised in glory: it is sown in weakness; it is raised in power: it is sown in a natural body; it is raised in spiritual body. The first Adam was a living soul; the last Adam was made a quickening spirit. Therefore, in order for us to learn the lesson we cannot remain with a earthly mindset like the 1st Adam but we must become obedient with a heavenly mindset like the 2nd Adam (Jesus). Transforming from a earthly mentality to a heavenly mentality will produce a level of maturity.

Notice how Christ handled His own suffering. Only by dealing with suffering as Christ dealt with it will that suffering cause you to mature. So what was the mindset of Jesus when He went through storms? When the pressure became very great on His life, He said, "Father...not my will, but yours be done." (Luke 22:42 NIV).

We have to do the same thing. When the pressure becomes great, do we say, "Father, not my will but yours." How many times have issues come up in our lives and we did opposite of the will of God?

Think about after the 9-11 tragedy when there were billboards all over the place stating "Pray for America." Now that time has passed, and we have gotten back into the routine of our normal lives, many of the billboards have been changed to some type of advertisement. America was wounded and hurt yet as a county we made an unspoken statement of unity "Father, not our will, but Your will be done." Well, America still needs pray but not just America but the entire world. Are we still praying for America and the entire world or have we done opposite of the will of God?

Jesus not only first asked for God's will when he faced hard times, He also spoke the word of God in trying times. When He was directly tempted by the Devil, Jesus never answered without using God's word. (See Matthew 4:1-11) The time has come to be determined to speak the word of God when you are facing temptations, especially when you realize you are facing Satan head on. No matter what he says or does, speak the Word in that instance.

Think about what Jesus did when he was on the boat in a horrendous storm. (See Matthew 8:24-27) He spoke to the

27

storm that was threatening to take his and the disciples' lives and that storm ceased its raging. Our application of the Word to our threatening storms should be like Christ's "Peace, be still" to those waves.

The reason some people don't speak the Word to their storms is because they are too weak to speak. You have heard the saying that knowledge is power, right? Never is that more true than when dealing with God's word. You are too weak to speak when you simply do not know God's word. How can you speak God's word over your circumstances if you have no idea what Gods' word says about your situation? When you know God's word, you can use it effectively in your situations, and it is through the word of God that the power comes for overcoming. Hebrews 4:12 tells us, "For the word of God is quick, and powerful, and sharper than any two-edged sword, piercing even to the dividing asunder of soul and spirit, and of the joints and marrow, and is a discerner of the thoughts and intents of the heart."(KIJ)

There's one more caveat to add here. I've already said that if you don't get the word of God in you, you won't have the knowledge to say what is written. Also, however, if you don't pray and spend time with God, you won't know how and when to use what Scriptures.

For example, I learn how to pronounce complicated medical terminology. However, without spending time studying through medical school and listening to the explanations of my professors, I will have no clue what these terms mean or when to use them. The relationship between Bible study and prayer is the same. You won't be mature enough to operate with the power you need to overcome your troubling situations unless you add prayer to the equation.

You see, there are some of you who do pray but experience no vitality in your prayer life because you are too stubborn to submit your will to Him. To pray with no vitality is to have an anemic prayer life. You're unable to distinguish living words from non-living words. When you speak out of hurt and pain, you speak death words and you won't have the power to survive. Your focus will be on the storm itself instead of on the purpose of the storm. The purpose is for you to grow, develop, and mature.

So now that you've lined up your suffering with God's word, how else will suffering help you to mature? Suffering causes you to mature when you line your life up with God's word. While you are experiencing suffering, and as you look back on suffering, be sure you live exactly as the Word tells you. You see, just because you know God's word that doesn't mean you are living it. Here are six things on which to concentrate as you line your life up with God's word.

#1: SELF-FOCUS

How long has the same issue come in your life over and over again and you still handle it the same way? Five, ten, fifteen, twenty, thirty, forty years has passed and you are still handling issues the same way. For you, perhaps it's always someone else's fault. You, blame others, get frustrated, and see other people's faults rather than focus on your own issues. Maybe you say damnable words to yourself and/or others.

I blamed my mother, Veronica, my biological father, David and my paternal grandmother, Esther, for years because none of them initially told me of my true identity. I found out by the mouth of another child. I was so focused on my own hurt and pain with hatred inside of me that I didn't realize the jewel

I had in my paternal grandmother. It wasn't until I was sitting at her viewing listening to the reflections from others about her life. Then I blamed myself because as an adult, I could have allowed myself the chance to get to know her as the others did. While sitting at the viewing and the funeral, I felt guilt because I had wasted time being held hostage in the pain of my past. If only I had given myself the opportunity to know her earlier on in my life. By the time, I allotted myself the opportunity to love and know her as my grandmother, I had only given myself seven years (1992-1999) and then she was gone. However, I am thankful for those years, because they taught me to daily do self-examination.

If you are facing a problem in your life, it's time for some self-focus. Deal with your issues. Stop venting your anger on others and do self-examination of your feelings and emotions. Out of control feelings and emotions are a sure sign that you are out of control. The purpose of doing self-examination is to test your faith so you will see exactly where you are. We're told in II Corinthians 13: 5-6 to examine ourselves as to whether we are in the faith. Test yourself. Do you not know yourself that Jesus Christ is in you?

It is also important that we be like David. In Psalms 26:2, he said, "Test me, O LORD, and try me, examine my heart and my mind." (NIV) David wanted the Lord to do an examination of him to see that his motives were right. How many times do you ask the Lord to do an examination of you to see if your motives and intentions are right? It is time for our temples to be clean because Christ is coming back for a church that is without spot, wrinkle, blemish or any such thing. (See Ephesians 5:27.)

#2: See That You're Saved

If you are not saved and you want to be a part of the Church for which Christ is coming, now is the time to accept Jesus Christ as your Lord and Savior. This is the most intelligent decision that you could ever make. The Spirit of God is ministering to you this very minute. *Come to Me and I will make you whole. You have suffered enough drama, now give Me your problems and let Me carry them for you. You have tried to do it your way long enough. I, Jesus, died for you that you might have life and have it more abundantly.*

Just say these words: I am a sinner, Jesus, and I acknowledge You, the son of God. I ask You to forgive me of my sins. I confess with my mouth and I believe in my heart that You died and arose just for me. I thank You for saving me and now I am a part of the family of God. I no longer belong to Satan and I am a son or a daughter of the Most High God. In Jesus' Name, Amen.

Now that you have accepted Jesus Christ into you life, I encourage you to find a church in your local area that is going to train you and teach you the Word of God. I beg of you to settle for nothing less, because it is the Word of God that is able to keep you from failing and present you faultless before the presence of His glory with exceeding joy.

#3: Stop Looking Only at the Issues

So many times we try replacing God instead of representing Him. You may ask, "But how do we replace God?" We replace God with our thoughts and opinions. We let our own thoughts and opinions replace what God would have us to think about our issues.

When you go through your issues, stop looking at the issue itself. Cast your eyes on Jesus. Put His face on the situation. See God in everything you do. When you remove God from your situation and place your feelings, emotions, intellect, and/or opinion on the situation, your actions are telling God, "I don't need You to tell me anything, I have this under control." Please realize that if you feel you have "it" or "yourself" under control, you are not letting God handle it; you are not under God's control.

Represent God, don't replace Him. God is able to handle your issues and He wants to take care of them for you. It's as if He's saying, "Give Me the chance to show you that you can represent Me. Don't try to handle your problems on your own without consulting Me. I know your thoughts before you realize them. Give Me your thoughts so I can direct you in the right path. Let Me lead you, my child. Don't replace Me, represent Me."

#4: Shun Hurtful Words from the Past

Maybe you have been abused in some way verbally, mentally, physically and/or sexually. Don't let the abuse stop you from going and growing in the Lord. You have no control over what people will do and say to you; however, their words can never come alive to you unless you accept what was said. I don't have a professional opinion or any statistics of this next statement but I believe when we accept other's words or actions, we literally pick up whatever they gave out and adopt it as the truth. Then we allow it to affect us, knowingly and unknowingly.

Maybe you were told as a child that you are just like your no-good father or mother. Perhaps someone said you will never be anything in life. If you accepted those words that were spoken to you and after a while started to believe those words, it may be very difficult for you to proceed in the Lord because this verbal abuse has now affected your self-esteem.

Maybe you were in a bad relationship. Negative things happened to you and you haven't been able to get over the drama nor the trauma that transpired. I encourage you this very day, to free yourself. Tell God how you are still hurting and ask Him to deliver you from the pain. Then forgive your abuser(s). Pray this prayer with me:

Father in the Name of Jesus, I ask You to heal me of my pain. God I am really hurting from these issues but I ask you to come into my life completely so that the pain will be released from me. God, I freely give you all issues concerning me. I cast my cares upon you. I cast down all imaginations that exalt themselves against You in my life. I pull down every hurtful event in the Name of Jesus that was designed to hinder me from reaching my destiny in You. I unleash every evil thing that was sent my way: fear, hatred, every negative word that was said over me, and the memory of every bad event that happened in my life. And I loose the resurrection power of Jesus Christ in my life. I declare soundness of mind, love, joy, and peace into my life. Lord, I, thank you that I am able to release my abuser(s), _____, into Your hands and I forgive _____ for everything that he/she put me through. Father, I thank you for setting me free in Jesus' name. Amen.

As a little girl, I remember the saying, "Sticks and stone can break my bones but words will never hurt me." It really sounded good saying that to someone who had said something to me that I didn't like. The question is, how about when I allow those words to hurt me? I accepted what was being said about me, and those words that were spoken tried (noticed I said tried) to hinder me from maturing in the Lord.

Words only hurt when we receive them instead of repel them. Proverbs 15:4 states, "A wholesome tongue is a tree of life...." The tongue should be used to speak positively into someone's life, not negatively. Once you allow the hurt from verbal abuse to be healed, learn from that and only let milk and honey be under your tongue. Milk represents nurturing words and honey represents sweet, kind, soft words. Allow your speech to be nurturing by speaking wisdom and saying soft words that are positive and give life such as thank you, you're welcome, please, honey, baby, etc., You get the point.

#5: Speak Life to Yourself

You may have been through some bad experiences, but I encourage you today to speak to your situation. The situation looks gloom and doom, and you don't understand why you have lost everything that belongs to you. Maybe you were an evacuee due to hurricanes Katrina and Rita. I still urge you to say like the psalmist, "I will lift up mine eyes unto the hills, from whence cometh my help. My help cometh from the LORD, which made heaven and earth." (Ps. 121:1-2 KJV)

Maybe you are on crack or some other illegal substance and your family has given up on you. Or you might have a loved one bound by the witchcraft demon of drug abuse. I want you to know there is still hope for you and your loved one. Your and their deliverance is in God. Speak to that crack demon or what-

34

ever demonic force that is dictating to that person's life. Serve that demonic force a notice from God that neither you nor your loved one will continue to be addicted. That spirit breeds in the mind; therefore, you must say, "My mind will not be affected by crack (or whatever demonic force is plaguing you). I shall have soundness of mind and I will not be held in bondage to this demonic force. I have been set free in the Name of Jesus." If you have a loved one struggling with demonic manifestations, continue to intercede for that person. Keep that person lifted up in prayer. Realize that what the Devil means for bad, God can turn for your good.

#6: ALLOW YOUR SUFFERING TO HELP YOU GROW

Maybe you didn't know your suffering in life could cause you to mature in the Lord, but now that you have been made aware of it, you are accountable for the knowledge you have obtained. To whom much is given, much is required. No more excuses such as, "Well, that's just the way I am." That mentality is only a blanket for you to cover up your mess and not deal with your issues. I'm informing you that you are held accountable for your actions.

I can share with you all of my hurts and pains from being abused, but the decision is still up to you to allow your suffering to cause you to mature in the Lord. It does not matter who hurt you, who lied on you, what you did to yourself to get you in the situation you are either in or just came out of. The thing that matters now is what you're going to do with the stuff that you have been through. Will you learn from it or will you dismiss it? Don't let anything or anybody stop you from going to the destined place God has prepared for you.

God allowed every situation to come your way. He could have stopped the situations from happening but He had a purpose in mind that needed to be fulfilled. He could have stopped me from being sexually abused as a child; however, He knew that I would mature in Him from that situation. He knew that it would cause me to have the mindset that no matter what state of affairs I faced, I would say, "It won't be this way always and this too shall come to pass." My suffering built within me the ability to look at a bad circumstance and say, "My situation is not what it looks like."

If you allow your suffering to teach you and cause you to mature in the Lord, you can be a tremendous asset to your brothers and sisters in the Lord because you will be able to help them grow. Proverbs 16:23 declares unto us, "The heart of the wise teacheth his mouth, and addeth learning to his lips." (KJV) Be wise and allow your heart to teach your mouth what to say, when to say it, and how to say it. In other words, let your heart educate your lips. If you don't understand what another person is going through or why he is doing whatever it is he is doing, close your mouth. That person may not like what he's doing, but due to some situation that has not been dealt with or resolved in his life, he is in the mess he's in. If you must open your mouth to say anything, pray for the person. Keeping your mouth shut about his situation, even though you feel you have the right to verbalize, and just praying instead can cause you to mature in the Lord.

There are many reasons why we suffer, but it is important for us to learn to mature in the Lord from our suffering. "Set your affection on things above, not on things on the earth." (Col 3:2, KJV) Put away the evil thoughts you have been harboring about those who hurt you or left you all alone. You may never know why you were adopted or why a catastrophic event happened to you. Some of you have evil passions and inordinate affections. Maybe you've been exposed to erroneous teachings or you have had abortions and have not forgiven yourself. For whatever reason you have suffered or are still suffering, let it go. Release it and articulate glory words for the rest of your life. Mature in the Lord in this way. The Scriptures tell us, "Let your speech be alway with grace, seasoned with salt, that ye may know how ye ought to answer every man." (Col 4:6, KJV) Having your vocabulary seasoned with salt will allow your words to cure and preserve that which you are speaking of or about. Permit your suffering to cause you to mature in the Lord. Maturity in the Lord will enable you to become secure in the Lord.

Chapter 3

Can I Be Secure in the Lord with All My Issues?

In I Peter 5:11, the word "stablished" means to be secure. The definition of secure is to be safe and free from risk of being intercepted. The only way we can be free from risk of being intercepted by distractions is to be stable in the Lord. Regardless of your past or present issues, you can be established, secure, and safe in the Lord. We have to realize, that our times are in His hands. No man can pluck us out of His hands. (See John 10:28-29.) Although in His hands, we jeopardize our fellowship with Him of our own doing, by way of our own free will and choices. We jump, leap, and run away from our base of security in Him when we allow ourselves to be distracted by life's problems. The moment has come for us to communicate to our issues and shout like the old hymn states, "On Christ the solid rock I stand; all other ground sinking sand." Also declare, "I will not be moved or shaken by my issues or problems because I am secure and safe in the Lord."

Surrender to Suffer

We can look at the apostle Paul as a good example of some-one who was secure in the Lord no matter what he went through. Hear Paul's own words:

> Are they servants of Christ? (I am out of my mind to talk like this.) I am more. I have worked much harder, been in prison more frequently, been flogged more severely, and been exposed to death again and again. Five times I received from the Jews the forty lashes minus one. Three times I was beaten with rods, once I was stoned, three times I was shipwrecked, I spent a night and a day in the open sea, I have been constantly on the move. I have been in danger from rivers, in danger from bandits, in danger from my own countrymen, in danger from Gentiles; in danger in the city, in danger in the country, in danger at sea; and in danger from false brothers. I have labored and toiled and have often gone without sleep; I have known hunger and thirst and have often gone without food; I have been cold and naked. Besides everything else, I face daily the pressure of my concern for all the churches.
>
> (2 Cor 11:23-28 NIV)

Yet through all of this, Paul was able to say in Acts 20:24, "But none of these things move me."

How is that kind of attitude possible? Paul spoke to Jesus about his issues. In 2nd Corinthians 12, Paul complained about his problems and in verse 9 Christ told him, "My grace is sufficient for thee: for my strength is made perfect in weakness." That's all Paul needed to hear. Then Paul said, "Most gladly therefore I will rather glory in my infirmities, that the power of Christ may rest upon me. Therefore I take pleasure in infirmities, in reproaches, in necessities, in persecutions, in distresses for Christ's sake: for when I am weak, then am I strong." You see, once Paul heard from the Lord, he was fine with whatever came his way. In order for Paul to converse such stalwart words, this brother had to be secure, established, and safe in Christ.

Now I realize that there are some people who have not reached the point of saying, "I will not be moved or shaken by my issues or problems." You are saying this because you don't feel secure and safe in the Lord. I want you to know that this chapter is especially for you.

God wants us to be healed and whole in Him. In the Bible, Jesus told a woman, "Your faith has made you whole." This woman had an issue. She was considered unclean and not worthy to be in public. In spite of her own fears and doubts or the opinions of people, she knew she had to get to Jesus. (See Matthew 9:20-22.)

The same thing applies to us today. Until we face our issues one on one, accept them, then deal with them, we will not be able to be secure in the Lord. We will be in denial about what is happening in our lives. Many Christians wear masks to cover up their problems. If you are a person who puts up a front around other people, I denounce the phoniness in your life in Jesus' Name. It is time for you, my Christian brother or sister, to be real.

Maybe you have been caught up in a generational curse. Things just keep repeating themselves in your family. You have the authority invested in you to break that curse. Jesus gave us the power and the authority to speak to our issues and say, "No more will you abide in my life, nor my children's lives, nor my children's children's lives." Maybe drug and alcohol addiction has been passed down to you through the family line. You have

41

the right given by Jesus to renounce that lifestyle out of your life.

You must realize that you are dealing with the manifestation of a spirit. Drug abuse is an offspring of witchcraft. The curse that needs to be broken isn't the drug abuse itself, it's witchcraft that needs to be broken. If we only cut the top of the weed off and never get to the root, it will grow up again. There is a product on the market called Weed Be Gone. This particular product kills the root of the weed. We need to start killing the demonic roots of the issues in our lives rather than always focusing on the manifestation.

There are many spirits (roots) and their manifestations (the tops of the weeds). We need to distinguish the spirit from the manifestations. Here is a list of a few spirits or roots and their manifestation:

When the root is <u>anger</u>, the manifestations are bickering, contention, being critical, disobedience, hatred, hostility, murders, rebellion, strife, and violence.

When the root is <u>death</u>, the manifestations are destruction of business, families and relationships, disease, and the urge to devour.

When the root is <u>deception</u>, the manifestations are confusion, craftiness, delusion, fantasy, hallucination, illusion, manipulation, mirages, and trickery.

When the root is <u>fear</u>, the manifestations are anxiety, confusion, depression, fantasy, lying, nervous breakdowns, paranoia, rejection, stress, timidity, and unbelief.

When the root is <u>greed</u>, the manifestations are covetousness, envy, evil desires, gluttony, grasping, indulgence, and intemperance.

When the root is <u>hell</u>, the manifestations are bankruptcy, begging, borrowing, debts, poverty, and starvation.

When the root is <u>hopelessness</u>, the manifestations are bitterness, defeat, despair, desperation, discouragement, inner pain, insanity, loneliness, resentment, self-destruction, withdrawal, and the tendency to be unyielding.

When the root is <u>idolatry</u>, the manifestations are compulsions, out-of-control desires or emotions, obsession, possessiveness, a willingness to follow other gods, and captivity to a persistent idea.

When the root is <u>lust</u>, the manifestations are adultery, fornication, homosexuality, lasciviousness, perversion, sexual abuse including masturbation, and uncleanness.

When the root is <u>pride</u>, the manifestations are arrogance, conceit, indifference to God's law, loftiness, lordliness, self-exaltation, self-love, self-pity, and unnatural affection.

When the root is <u>witchcraft</u>, the manifestations are compulsions, drug abuse, financial bondage, occult bondage, and rebellion. This root bewitches, captivates, charms, controls, deadens, desensitizes, enchants, entices, lures, and numbs your spirit, making it, perhaps, the most dangerous root indeed.

By knowing the difference between the spirits (roots) and their manifestations, we will be empowered to deal with our issues effectively. We will know exactly what is in operation in our lives. This will also help us in spiritual warfare. We will know what spirit to bind in our lives as well as in someone else's life. We can do self-examination and see what manifestations we have in our lives, then curse the root.

Once we deal with, confront, and resolve the issues in our lives, we are no longer held captive them. We will no longer be victims but we will be victorious. Psalms 147:3 states, "He heals the brokenhearted and binds up their wounds." (NIV) Ah, that's good news. All we have to do is give Him our broken hearts and He will bandage, protect, immobilize, compress, and support them. Whether the hurt was self-inflicted or caused by another, it doesn't matter. Just give Him your broken heart so you can be healed and made whole and complete.

I remember as a child having a broken heart filled with hatred. I was withdrawn because I did not understand why certain things were happening to me. I used to say, "I didn't do anything. Why is this happening?" I had to go through all of the events in my life so I could help someone else with their issues.

Let's gaze at my life. From birth to age six, I was a happy little girl. I was taught Raymond is my daddy. At the age of seven, I became aware of my biological father, David. I was molested from age eight until I was 16 by a deputy sheriff, an uncle by marriage. The one who protects the law was the one violating the law. At age 16, I was saved and filled with the Holy Ghost. I came to understand that God had chosen me to minister His Word, but I was 16 and I had a boyfriend, Kent. By age 17, I was a mother of a baby girl, Nikeah (Nikki).

I graduated from Mardela High School at age 18, got pregnant again, had an abortion, and needed anti-depressant pills to cope with what I had done. I felt I couldn't have this baby because I already had one and my boyfriend had another girl pregnant at the same time. I wanted to pursue my education at Norfolk State University and major in accounting, but I was a mother so my plans had to change. Instead, I attended Woodridge Business Institute in Salisbury, Maryland, for accounting.

By the age of 19, I was engaged and my boyfriend (yes, the same guy) was in the United States Army serving in Germany. In my mind, everything was going to be all right. I forgave him for getting the other girl pregnant, but told him he had only one more time to hurt me like that and it was going to be over. So there he was, in Germany serving our country, and two months before our wedding, I discovered that he is living there with another woman. The engagement was over.

By now I was 20-years-old and I backslid from God because I had been hurt too many times. My attitude said, *I just can't take it any more.* I was still going to church every Sunday, but my mind wasn't into the services. I started going to the club with the girls and hoping I wouldn't get carded.

By age 21, I was in and out of clubs and I had a new boyfriend, James (Jay), who was a deejay. For the first six months of the relationship, everything was beautiful. There were no arguments and we went places and did things together. I figured that things were looking up. I began to feel that God had blessed me because my heart was telling me so. This man was a radio personality at a widely-listened-to station in late 1980's. He was popular and a good person, but he was not saved even though he had a church background. At the seven-month mark in our relationship, I find out that he had a substance abuse problem.

Meanwhile, remember, I was a church girl and knew nothing about the arena which I had entered; however, I thought I could help change him. (Take it from someone who had to learn the hard way because I wouldn't listen, young ladies, never, ever, ever think you can change a man. You can't do it, so don't even try.)

Well, we moved together and the substance abuse became more dominant in his life. He got fired from his job at the radio station. We decided to relocate to the Washington, D.C. metropolitan area, so I quit my job at Henson Airlines trying to help my man. We moved and I naively thought the drug couldn't follow us to the other side of the Chesapeake Bay Bridge. After all, it was a new area and we knew very few people there. I felt this was the perfect little plan. No more drugs. Everything is going to be just fine.

I was 22-years-old now and I found out that I was pregnant again. I also found out that somehow drugs had found my man in Landover, Maryland. I didn't understand. I was thinking, *He doesn't know any drug dealers in the area. Why is this happening, he left the drug scene on the Eastern Shore.* I wasn't familiar with spirits and their manifestations.

I started stressing out about having this new baby, but before I gave birth, the doctor in Princess George's County General Hospital in Cheverly, Maryland gave me the news that I had 24 to 48 hours to live due to toxemia. I had almost stressed myself to death. This taught me that the phrase, "you worry me to death" is not just a figure of speech; it can be reality if you let it. I had to be sent to Francis Scott Key Hospital in Baltimore for an emergency c-section, and I gave birth during the 7th month of my pregnancy to a 2 lb., 9.8 oz baby girl, Kierra.

The trauma wasn't over, though. A few days after my daughter's birth, the doctor and nurses rushed in my room because my blood pressure was soaring. I should have had a stroke. In my backslidden state, I heard God tell me, "You shall live and not die, I still have work for you to do." I remember the nurse putting a pill under my tongue and helping me to lie on my left side, a position from which I could not move for a period of time. Finally, my blood pressure lowered and I was released from the hospital.

At age 23 I had another abortion. I just couldn't have another baby and I didn't even bother to tell my boyfriend that I was pregnant. By this time, he had supposedly changed. He moved back to the Eastern Shore to get himself together, got a job at WESM at the University of Maryland Eastern Shore, and found a place for us to live. I moved back to the Eastern Shore and by age 24 was pregnant again. Unfortunately I ended the relationship with him because the substance abuse problem arose again.

I moved in with my maternal grandparents, Jason and Gertrude, with two children and another on the way. This was overwhelming me, so I made an appointment to go get another abortion. I was informed that it would cost me $400 and that was the exact amount of money I had. However, the cousin, Tyronna, that I'd asked to take me decided the day before to call the abortion clinic and found out that I needed an extra $100 because I was farther along in the pregnancy than I thought. I didn't have another hundred dollars and couldn't ask anyone to give me the money. She wasn't going to lend it to me. Yet, I had another cousin, Monique, who kept telling me, "Vanda, these kids are a blessing to you." Not having that $100 forced me to go through with the pregnancy and give birth to my son, Trevon.

All these ups and downs turned me back to God. I re-established my relationship with my Heavenly Father and moved into my own place with my kids. At age of 25, I met a state trooper, Ernest. He was a nice guy, wasn't on drugs, had his own place, loved to cook, and went to church. There was just one hitch, he had a girlfriend. When he told me things weren't working out between them, instead of letting him go, I hung around. We had fun together and my hopes began to lift. Then I find out he was getting married. Fooled again.

To add to my misery, my home that I was renting caught on fire. The damage was total. We had almost nothing left but the clothes that the four of us had on that day, December 17th. The only other thing that didn't get burned up in the fire was a Thompson Chain Reference Bible I had been given by Minister Reginald & Marla Morris. I still use that Bible to this day and I'm thankful that they were obedient to sow that seed into my life. Of course, my children and I had to move back in with my grandparents.

By age 26, I had another place of my own in Salisbury, Maryland. In April of that year, I met a guy, Matt, who was a very nice person, wasn't on drugs, and had his own place with roommates. On our first date, we went to a church service. However, he wasn't saved, but every now and then he would go to church with me. I figured the relationship was really progressing because we would go to Painter, Virginia, to visit his mom. In November, the seventh month of our relationship, I moved back to my hometown of San Domingo. I noticed when I moved back there that we didn't see each other as often although we continued to talk until December 31st.

That evening, I remember God asking me a question. "How long will you stay with this man knowing he doesn't want to serve Me?" That question gave me the determination to resolve that if he didn't want God then I wasn't going into the next year with him. This was hard for me because I really liked this guy and my kids liked him.

I asked him to come to my house that evening. I told him he had to show up before 10 pm because I would be going to church that night. When he arrived, I asked him, "Are you ready for a one-on-one relationship with God?"

He told me, "No, I'm not ready for that right now."

It was one of the hardest things I ever had to do, but I felt that I had to let him go. I knew God was ready to bless me, but if this man didn't want God to be first in his life, and I hung onto him, he would block my blessings. At that New Year's Eve service, I remember crying out to God saying, "I want to serve You and I want to do what You want me to do." Then Bishop Catherine Camper of United Deliverance Bible Center in Laurel, Deleware, sang a song that just blessed me. She sang, "I still have joy, I still have joy, after all the things that I've been through, I still have joy." After that, those words went with me everywhere I went. I was tired of one relationship ending entering another within months. I had to realize my joy was in God. I was tired and was ready for a change in my life. I was ready for God to take over in my life. I finally, seriously surrendered to His will.

By this time, I was 27-years-old. I faced the fact that this man, although he was a friend whom I could talk to about anything and who could talk to me, was a friend who needed Jesus in his life. He was in a backslidden state. Then he accepted Jesus back into his life.

A few months later, during a service at Bishop George Copeland's church, United Faith of Deliverance, in Salisbury, Maryland God used Prophet Todd Hall to minister to me about my past. Prophet Hall showed me how God took the first man I was supposed to marry out of the country so that I wouldn't marry him. He went on, though, to tell me that I would get married that year and would go through the marriage for Him. He said God was saying, "What you go through in this marriage will help others to see Me no matter what you or they go through. You are called my evangelist." I knew the message was from God because it was so exact and detailed. The details included portions of my life I was certain no one else knew about me. The prophecy was confirmation of what God had already told me.

On October 29th of that year, William Jenkins Jr. and I, YoVanda Brown, became one. We were Mr. and Mrs. Jenkins. (I's married now!). Our blended family became a real family—he with his son, Tyrell, and me with my three kids.

I thought a husband would sooth the inner pain that I couldn't speak about. I would no longer have to hop from relationship to relationship. Finally there would be some stability in my life. I had my own husband. However, this relationship was something different, something that was supposed to be permanent, and I had to focus on keeping it real.

Little did I realize, though, that a wedding doesn't make a marriage. We had both entered the relationship with unresolved issues with which we soon had to deal. Coming to this realization was when the pyrotechnics of our connection came alive. I'm not talking about the fireworks of making love even though we were legal and we had license for the sex drive. I'm talking about dealing with each other, facing the issues head on in order to become a brilliant display. In order for virtue to literally come out of us, we would have to allow the works of the fire of the Holy Spirit to refine the impurities out of us. The adversities we faced made each other grow; he pushed me and I pushed him. Where I was weak, he was strong and vice versa. Through those times, we learned to keep it real with each other.

By age 28, I thought I had completely accepted the fact that I had been sexually abused until God decided to use my husband to minister to me about it. I actually got mad because no one knew before then. I had carefully hid and neatly covered up that part of my life and I was angry to see that God would show that private part of me to him.

Shortly after getting mad with my husband because of what God had revealed to him about me, I went to a Sunday School Seminar at St. Matthews First Baptist Church of Laurel, Deleware. Sister Deborah Brinkley was conducting the seminar. The Spirit of God came in and she did a shift in the spirit realm.

God used her to minister to me about the deep hurts from my past. She said that God wanted to heal me and make me whole from what had been done in secret. He had others out there waiting on me, to hear what He brought me through, to hear how He would do the same for them. In my mind, I was wondering how we switched from the original topic of the seminar to be talking about my life. I didn't want to deal with the fact that all those terrible things had actually happened to me. I thought, *I'm fine, God, just let it alone.*

But God wanted me to be healed and I wouldn't accept it when He used my husband to expose it. You see, God will get what He wants when He has a purpose in mind for you. It took until nine months after the seminar, but I finally said to God, "OK if this is what you want, then you tell me to share it."

A mere two days later, Evangelist Sadie Brunson from Wilmington, Deleware, was leading a revival at my home church. It was a Sunday afternoon and I walked past her in the church hall. She gently touched my hand and said, "There are some things that God said it is time for you to share."

I just looked at her and shook my head. I said, "OK, God, I am willing; I know this is You." I then informed my family about what God was leading me to do. The first thing I did was confront my abuser. I guess this tipped the Devil off that I was serious about moving into what God had planned for me. Since this was not only the first step in my own deliverance, but was also the first step in my attacking his kingdom by reaching out to help effect the deliverance of others, the Devil got real mad. The first counterattack came when my husband relapsed into alcohol and drug use.

I was 29 when our family was instructed by God to move to another church. We began attending The United Deliverance Bible Center in Laurel, Deleware. Bishop Dr. Catherine Camper is founder and was pastor then with her Assistant Pastor, Dr. Keith Wongus. Dr. Wongus and his wife, Pastor Carla, are currently pasturing there. I answered yes to the call God had on my life. From then until the present, I have been living as an anointed, Godly wife, working in the ministry, and helping and encouraging those who were hurting, discouraged, or otherwise in need.

In August of 2000, God instructed me to work in the ministry with my biological father, Pastor T. David Hackett at Trinity United Methodist Church Community Worship Center in Princess, Maryland. I was there until the birth of Oasis Living Word Ministries on April 14, 2001. I, YoVanda Jenkins, serve as pastor where Pastor Bruce Parham, now bishop, officiated the ordination.

Oasis began to grow. We outgrew the first unit we were leasing in Fruitland, Maryland, and moved to Delmar, Maryland in April 2002. Then on April 13, 2003, my husband was ordained and we began to pastor together. We outgrew that location and moved to Salisbury in January 2004.

I thank God for the way my life has turned out thus far. I know the best is yet to come, good God from Zion. I believe we haven't seen anything yet.

If I hadn't experienced the issues that came into my life the way they happened, I wouldn't be able to minister effectively about suffering. Now I thank God for the stress, the hardships, and the adversities that have come my way. The Bible tells us, "In every thing give thanks." (I Thess. 5:18 KJV) It also tells us, "...neither be ye sorry; for the joy of the LORD is your strength." (Neh. 8:10 KJV) Thanks to these circumstances in my life, my measure of faith was increased.

I knew that God was able to deliver me and forgive me. The hardest part came when I had to forgive myself for having two abortions and three children before I was married. Many times I had thoughts that no man would want me with three kids, at least no one would want to marry me anyway. Sometimes I still have to remind myself of what my cousin, Monique, told me years ago; my children are blessings from God. God had still blessed me even with my past.

One day at work, a lady sat down at my desk and I knew she was a lesbian. She was bold and open about it, so I asked her why she had decided to live as a lesbian? She proceeded to tell me that her father molested her until she was 15-years-old. He only stopped then because she ran away from home. She simply couldn't take his doing that to her anymore. Since that time in her life, she had no desire to be with a man. When she left my desk, I got up, went into the lady's room and just worshipped God. I was thankful to God because that could have been me. I could have been so emotionally scarred to the point that I would not have affections for a man.

Still, I had to face other manifestations from being molested. The molestation was the reason why I hopped from relationship to relationship. I was feeding the spirit of lust that had been deposited in me from being violated as a child. Then I struggled for years getting delivered from that lust spirit in the manifestation of masturbation.

Masturbation was my friend. I was well trained in hiding and covering up secrets all my life, so I hid this little habit too. I didn't see anything wrong with it. It wasn't fornication. Preachers preached on fornication and I had been convicted of that plenty of times.

However, I later learned that a strong desire to have sex with oneself is evil concupiscence which is listed as a sin in Colossians 3:5. I was made aware that masturbation is mating with a demonic force of like gender. Well, I had no desire to be intimate with another woman. I had to realize that something was wrong with the idea of my lusting on me. There is nothing heterosexual about masturbation; it's sex with the same sex, me with me, and that makes it a homosexual act.

I remember still struggling with masturbation in the early years of my marriage. When my husband would leave home for days due to the spirit of witchcraft in the manifestation of drug addiction in his life, I was hurt and lonely. In that dark place, I needed my "friend;" that's where I found comfort. I knew to pray or could have called someone to pray for me, but I desired my "friend." I wasn't ready to expose this manifestation so that the root could be killed. I enjoyed my "friend," but I knew it was a hindrance to my walk in Christ. I had to make a choice.

I had to be ready to let that friend die. I was seated in heavenly places and this challenge had to be mortified. I praise God that I have indeed been healed and made whole over that spirit of lust and the manifestation of masturbation is no longer a part of my life.

In 1998, a woman approached me and said I was hurting because of my husband's addiction. Although she was persistent, I knew I wasn't hurting about that. I had been well equipped in the characteristics of the mindset of a dominating homosexual manifestation. I knew that manifestation preys on the vulnerability of a hurting victim. The lust spirit came back to test my faith, to see if I would break. Remember, my "friend" was dead, so the same familiar spirit moved toward me but with a new face. So I had to let Lust know I was not hurting and he could do nothing for me. My husband would take care of every need, want, or desire that I had. At first, I was offended that the spirit approached me through the woman, but I had to remember righteousness isn't pure if it hasn't been tested.

The Bible tells us to let the strong bear the infirmities of the weak. (See Romans 15:1.) It also states that when you are strengthened, strengthen your brethern.(See Luke 22:32.) I encourage you to do like Jesus did and show your wounds. I have shown you my wounds; someone is waiting to hear and see what you have been through. Show them your medals of honor.

Our bruises and scars serve to display the magnificence of the delivering power of God. They are also to remind us where we came from so that we don't forget. They enable us to go and witness to our brothers and sisters who are still in the mess that we came out of by the grace of God. We are not brothers and sisters in Christ because of our skin; we are kin because of the sin that is within. Both our saved and unsaved brothers and sisters need to be strengthened. Don't be afraid to show your wounds or to see the wounds of others. What appears to be a sight no one should ever see, is the very thing you need to show.

Someone needs to know that you have been violated sexually, even if it was by someone in church leadership and they told you to keep quite about it.

Someone needs to know that you had to give your baby up for adoption.

Someone needs know that you were suicidal for whatever reason.

Someone needs to hear that you had an affair outside of your marriage.

Solomon let us know that there is nothing new under the sun. (See Eccl. 1:9.)

What has happened to you—your trips, your falls, your mistakes—are nothing new, and you have been delivered in order to let someone else know he can live through it. Don't get weak now because your sin has been exposed. Free yourself and others by showing your wounds when God tells you to do so.

God wants us to be secure in Him regardless of our past and/or current issues. He has a purpose in mind to be fulfilled and He wants to use your life, with all its issues, to accomplish that purpose. Once you have been established in Him, then you will be strengthened and equipped for the work of the ministry.

Chapter 4

Why Do Trials Come My Way?

How many times have you asked the big question, "Why am I having these trials?" I know I've asked time and time again. Well, believe it or not, your trials have a purpose and will lead you to your destiny if you allow them to. The anointing on your life is not a blockade for the trials, it's the very reason they are coming your way.

Trials come to make us strong. In 1 Peter 5:10, Peter encourages the believers to whom he is writing by telling them that God's strength will follow suffering. And Peter should know. Jesus told Peter straight out, "And the Lord said, Simon, Simon, behold, Satan hath desired to have you, that he may sift you as wheat: But I have prayed for thee, that thy faith fail not: and when thou art converted, strengthen thy brethren (Luke 22:31-32, KJV).

Since Jesus hasn't changed and He's still no respecter of persons, the same thing applies to us today when we face a difficult task or trial that challenges our faith. The Devil wants to sift us as wheat too, but we cannot allow our faith to fail. We need our faith. No matter how the Devil tries to sift us, if our faith fails, we're giving up, effectively giving ourselves to his clutches. For the sake of our spiritual survival, we must stay strong and not let go of our faith.

Even with that said, there still will come times in your life when you will feel like throwing in the towel or giving up because all hope seems to be gone; however, realize that Satan wants you to remain distracted by your circumstances. He wants to place fear in your life. Wouldn't it be great to have a safe haven to run to while going through so as not to get sideswiped by your problems?

In 1 Kings 1:50-53, Adonijah was afraid of his brother Solomon. He felt his hope was gone because he, not his brother, was supposed to be king of Israel. Due to his fears, he knew he needed to be in a holy place, so he took hold of the horns of the altar for safety. He figured no one was so calloused as to kill him while he hung on to God's altar. Adonijah was right in running to God. Solomon indeed did not kill him.

How many times do we seek the face of God when our fears come upon us or when we have been stripped of something that we felt was rightly ours? Instead of seeking God, what we sometimes do is give in to our fears by allowing spirits and their manifestations to rule and reign in our lives.

It is time for us to take a stand against the things that trouble us. For too long, we have fretted and allowed ourselves to operate in fear because someone might get our position or someone might get more recognition than what we get. Brother or Sister XYZ might pledge more than we have to give, or the pastor might recognize someone else after the service and say nothing to me.

We actually allow ourselves to be troubled by such dumb stuff, and in the house of God. So what if you don't get the position you thought was yours. So what if that man or woman married someone else. Wake up and get over it. God has something else for you that's far greater than the dumb stuff.

Grab the horns of the altar. There is too much work to do in the Kingdom of God for you to be intimidated and bound by fear over petty stuff. Enough time has been wasted. Your trials cannot make you strong if you insist on grovelling in them. Push through them. Straining against weight builds muscle. You will never be strong by lying under them.

One of the things you can do to build spiritual muscle is to get to work in God's vineyard. Luke 10:2 tells us that the harvest is ripe but the laborers are few. God has so much work available that some of the ripe fruit is rotting while waiting because the laborers are few. I have asked the question, "Lord, why are the laborers few?" His reply to me was, "The little foxes are destroying the vine. The laborers are letting little things hinder them from reaching the harvest. They are working; however, their employer is Problems. The rate of their pay is worry. Their bonus is frustrations. Their y.t.d., year-to-date intake is stress."

On the other hand, how many times do people use the altar as a blanket to make it appear to others that they are in right standing with God? Every Sunday, they are at the altar for the same thing, knowing that their intent is not to let the problem go. They are seeking attention because they didn't get what they thought was theirs.

Please, don't get me wrong. I'm not referring to the people who want to do good in their heart but evil is always present. They want to do the things of God but have not matured in a particular area so they keep going to the altar. I encourage them to keep going until they get their breakthrough.

I am talking to those whose motive it is set on being deceptive, seeking to obtain a title without having the heart of a servant. This type of person is out to promote the kingdom of self, not the Kingdom of God.

Adonijah, Solomon's half-brother was one of these types. He approached Bathesheba, Solomon's mother, and said he was coming to her peaceably, when peace was far from his intent. He exalted himself and said, "I will be King" (1 King 5:5). He attempted to usurp the throne and wanted Abishag, David's young lovely servant-nurse, to be his wife.

I King 2:15-23 covers this interesting story. Adonijah started out being sarcastic. "You know that the kingdom was mine, and all Israel had set their expectations on me, that I should reign." In other words, he was saying *I am to be King according to the people.* How many times has man put man in a position and God never said that this person was the man for the position? Still in a sarcastic tone, Adonijah continued, "However, the kingdom has been turned over, and has become my brother's for it was his from the Lord." He felt that which he thought was his had been stripped from him. Then he threw in the family feud and power struggle that existed in both the biological and spiritual family and he was clearly not in agreement with the Lord's decision. He wanted the authority for himself, but understood God's authority. After all, his own name meant Jehovah is my Lord.

Adonijah went on, "Now I ask one petition of you; do not deny me." He had gotten his feelings off his chest then felt obligated to manipulate and control Bathsheba, his opponent's mother. He figured she had sat, heard his anger, and understood why he had every right to be bitter. He'd been violated; therefore, somebody owed him for his pain and suffering. He'd selected her to be his victim.

Bathsheba listened. She was naïve of the control that her son's brother was working on her because she thought he had come in peace. "Then he said, please speak to King Solomon for he will not refuse you, that he may give me Abishag the Shumannite as wife." When a person is naïve and the controller uses soft gentle words such as peace, it is hard for the naïve person to believe that she's being controlled because the controller appears to be presenting himself in peace. The mind-set of the controller is *I'm going to get me—me, get whatever, whomever, whenever, however, and wherever by any means necessary by using whomever is available to be used—mother, father, brother, grandparents, aunts, uncles, cousins—it doesn't matter.*

Because Bathsheba was the mother of Solomon, Adonijah felt he could use her position in her son's life to get what he wanted. The controller always seeks for power and authority to rule and reign in their on kingdom of selfishness. Abishag was young, beautiful, a virgin, and a servant/nurse of David. Since Adonijah didn't get to rule Israel, there was a driving desire in him to be head of something or somebody, whether his victim desired him or not.

"So Bathsheba said, very well, I will speak for you to the king." Her husband, David, had recently died, so Adonijah used her at a time when she was distracted by her emotions. She was without a husband and Abishag was without a job. That may have sounded like a good plan; however, Adonijah must have forgotten that his brother was a wise man.

Solomon did not fall to the spirit of deception. He recognized that the voice of his mother wasn't actually her speaking. That's why Solomon asked, "Why do you ask for Abishag for Adonijah?" Solomon was wise to the trickery of his brother and that is why Solomon ordered Adonijah's execution.

You see, Adonijah was angry because he felt he had been dealt with unfairly. He was hurting. Instead of letting his trial help him, he tried to handle it on his own, but he obviously went about it all-wrong.

Like Adonijah, there are people in this world who are hurting and have not dealt with their pain. Some don't know how to deal with their pain, so they take it out on other people. Pain that has not been dealt with turns into anger. Uncontrolled anger produces rage. Rage causes a person to act in a verbally and/or physically violent manner.

This discussion brings us back now to the original point of this chapter which is the fact that our trials make us strong. When we face our trials, certain things within us are tested. For example, if God needs to show us that we have anger issues, He may allow pain in our lives. That pain then displays warning signs before anger is full blown. If we ignore the warning signs like irritation, frustration, moodiness, low temperance, and being overemotional and easily provoked, anger can take us over. When we feel within our spirit that our flesh is being taken over by that anger and is getting out of control, we need to learn how to discipline that feeling. The only way any of our feelings can become disciplined is by developing a lifestyle of fasting, praying, and worshipping God.

Fasting will allow us to keep our flesh under subjection; praying will keep us in communication with God, and worshipping Him will allow us to take our minds off of us and put it on Him. Worshipping God takes us above the pain and sits us in heavenly places right here on earth. Through fasting, prayer, and worship, we are able to obtain strength.

Our strength is also taken in several other ways. I Samuel 28:20 says of Saul, "...there was no strength in him; for he had no bread all day or all night." I understand that some of you will never have your strength zapped due to not eating; however, we have some brothers and sisters who are not able to eat when trails/situations come their way. The problem comes and the appetite goes. This trick is a set-up. The ultimate goal of our appetite leaving is that the Devil wants our strength to be zapped. If we are weak, how will we be alert to and aware of Satan's devices? He is cunning.

I was snookered with this trick. Sometimes you have to physically speak to situations in your life. I had to say to my problem, "You may come, but I am going to eat." I am still working on this thing; my strength will not be zapped and I will eat. I am going to tell the truth and expose the Devil. Come what may, I'm going to eat.

According to Psalms 31:10, David said, "...my strength faileth because of mine iniquity." Sin also will drain our strength and sexual looseness is a strength-zapping sin we fall into all too often. Proverbs 31:3 says, "Give not they strength unto women." Women carry a lot of power between their thighs, and if that power is used inappropriately, men will be ruined. Men, you must realize how much strength God has implanted in you. If you release your seed into a woman who is not your wife, you are setting yourself up be destroyed. Silly women don't care about commitment; they only seek for pleasure–a temporary fix. Let me tell you something else about these women; they seek for men who let the wrong head lead them. Word to the wise: married men, if you want to be strengthened, give due benevolence to your wife. In other words, get your groove o-o-n-n with your wife!" (That's my translation of 1 Cor. 7:3.)

Psalms 71:9 says, "Cast me not off in the time of old age, forsake me not when my strength faileth." Age is another component that has its way of dimensioning our strength; nevertheless, I encourage every father and mother in the Lord to continue to allow your lives to be examples to those who cross your path. God has allowed you to go through many situations and grow through them so that you may enhance those younger than you coming along.

I am ever so grateful for a father in the Lord who shared his life's experiences with me. I remember one Sunday afternoon between services when he sat beside me and started sharing his views on the pros and cons about marriage. I knew he had the experience to speak on the issue since he had been married for 50 some years and I wasn't married at the time nor was I thinking about getting married. I thank God for what the late Deacon Leon, a.k.a. Deac, from St. Matthews poured into my life before leaving this earth. He was a man of great wisdom. Once I got married, I asked the Lord to bring back to my remembrance what Deac had said. It became evident to me that there was a purpose for his sharing that information with me. I encourage everyone to encourage our fathers and mothers in the Lord and to listen to what they have to say. Pray for their strength. They are not all old and feeble. They have purpose.

Daniel was left alone in Daniel 10:8 and saw a great vision. Afterward, no strength remained in him. When the anointing is very heavy on us, it physically weakens our bodies. Our frail bodies can only absorb so much of the glory of God at a time. When you pour out what God has birthed in your spirit man, your physical body gets weak and without being covered with prayer, you are setting yourself up for unnecessary attacks. Men and women of God, train those under you to lift you up in prayer. It is for this reason that men and women of God cannot get beside themselves when the Lord works mightily through them. It's easy to think they are all that, but must realize that whatever happened was not their own doing or abilities. It is through God that we move, live, and have our being. That's why it is very important to have armor bearers.

I encourage all armor bearers to know your place and stay in your position. Meanwhile, pray, pray, pray, and keep praying for your headship. Anything less than full submission is rebellion. Obstacles will be presented in your life to take your strength to stop you from praying.

Regardless of what comes our way to attempt to dissipate our strength, we have to know and believe that trials do come to make us strong. Therefore, refuse to let deception, anger, a lifestyle without fasting, praying and worshipping, the inability to eat or overeating due to pressure, sexual looseness, old age or a non-prayer life for your spiritual leader weaken you. Then when you are strengthened, it want be as hard to understand being restored from our suffering.

Chapter 5

Will I Ever Be Restored from My Suffering?

We have been dealing with In 1 Peter 5:10 throughout this book and now we come to the final phrase. Again, the verse says, "But the God of all grace, who hath called us unto his eternal glory by Christ Jesus, after that ye have suffered a while, make you perfect, stablish, strengthen, settle you" (KJV). To settle you means God has already decided what situations to let us face in order for us to be restored. It had already been agreed upon between the Father, the Son, and the Holy Spirit before our substance had even been formed that we were going to be settled. We can follow this point from what is stated in Genesis 1:26 "Let Us make man in Our image, according to Our likeness." Since we are made according to the likeness of the Trinity, and in the Trinity there are no spots, wrinkles, blemishes or any such things, then we can deduce that the Trinity is settled; therefore, our being settled is a foregone conclusion. God wants us to be restored to the condition of the way He created the first Adam before the fall.

Before the Fall of Man, Adam enjoyed perfect communion with God, freedom from Satan, no sickness, a home in the garden, and dominion. Man and animals had fellowship and many more benefits. Thanks to the Fall, we lost all of that and instead obtained, separation from God, servanthood to sin, sickness and disease, death, damnation to hell, and much more. This is why we need to be settled and restored in order to bring us back to His original plan for our lives.

This brings us to the question of the title of this chapter, "Will I ever be restored from my suffering?" The answer is a resounding, "Yes, if you want to be restored." To be restored means that which was lost will be regained so beautifully that it won't even be noticeable that loss was ever suffered in the first place. In other words, the now is so revitalized that the loss becomes not a painful memory to be forgotten, but a tool for witnessing.

If I can come to understand my suffering in this new light, I can see that to *surrender to suffer* is not a sign of weakness. My surrendering to my suffering does not mean that I am throwing in the towel, quitting, or ceasing to believe. I now understand that surrender means to submit. I am yielding my power and my will to the will of God. Submission is an attitude of the mind, which is caused by obedience and humility. I therefore submit myself to learn whatever lessons God has for me to learn through my suffering.

One type of suffering is physical sickness. There are times in our lives when we are physically ill and it seems like our health will not be restored. However, the Word of God tells us in Jer. 30:17–"For I will restore health to you, and heal you of your wounds, says the Lord. Because they called you a castout

68

saying: 'This is Zion; no one seeks her.'" There is someone who has been sick for a long time and you have been called a castout. You have accepted that I might get healed. This sickness is not unto death. My brother and/or my sister you need to recite this Scripture every day until it gets in your spirit that God will restore health to you. Faith comes by hearing and hearing comes by hearing the Word. However, there is someone that is sick unto death and this is not a bad thing. Christians do die of illnesses but they spend eternity with the Lord. That is our ultimate restoration.

The Bible states in 1 Sam. 15:22, "Behold, to obey is better than sacrifice." To sacrifice is to give an offering unto God or a false god. We cannot supersede the ultimate sacrifice, which was Christ's, so no matter how much we give, we can't beat what God has given. However, our obedience is an act of sacrifice and worship, which states to Him that we are willing to lay down our time, money, abilities, talents, readiness. or desire to do, as well as our wants, dreams, desires, passions, motives, feelings, and ways in order to accept all that He has to offer us. It is truly sacrificial obedience when we are willing to lay any of this down even if we have to suffer to reach the place where God wants us to be.

Paul had to show the church of Corinth about sacrificing to truth versus to what is false in the eleventh chapter of Second Corinthians. In being restored, you have to be honest with people the way Paul was honest with this church. Consider II Cor. 11:1–4:

Oh, that you would bear with me in a little folly—and indeed you do bear with me. For I am jealous for you with godly jealousy. For I have betrothed you to one husband, that I may present you as a chaste virgin to Christ. But I fear, lest somehow, as the serpent deceived Eve by his craftiness, so your minds may be corrupted from the simplicity that is in Christ. For if he who comes preaches another Jesus whom we have not preached, or if you receive a different spirit which you have not received, or a different gospel which you have not accepted—you may well put up with it! (NKJ)

Paul was saying, "Let me be straight up with you, man to man, woman to woman. I know you can handle me being a little foolish because you are showing me you are familiar with foolishness. What you are doing is hurting me to my heart. I promised to give you in marriage to one husband, Jesus Christ, but you've been tricked into having an affair with another. Satan, who is skilled in underhandedness and is deceiving you, so that your mind becomes extremely objectionable from the modest behavior that is in Christ."

Paul was telling them that if they entertain someone who is giving you heresy (half-truths) and they can't discern what they are being told, they might as well sit there and be underhanded themselves. Paul was upset. He knew the Corinthian believers should have known better. He had spent quality time teaching them the truth and not for pay, so they would know the truth and not be deceived. Yet, although they knew better, they put up with foolishness gladly. They should have been mature enough to be the teachers, but instead they were entertaining spirits. They were acting like babies, drinking milk when they should have been eating meat. How did they let their minds take them back to a childish mentality?

When you fall back into whining about your suffering and listening to what everybody else is telling you instead of what God's word is telling you, you are acting just like the Corinthians. God wants to restore you. Stop looking at your problem and mediating on it. Instead, allow your eyes to see farther than what is actually in front of you. You've got to see your suffering in the spiritual realm and stop looking at things foolishly.

How many times have we been given truth and yet our minds became extremely objectionable from the simplicity that is in Christ? I'm not talking about the babe in Christ. I'm talking about the mature one–the Holy-Ghost-filled, fired-baptized, speaking-in-tongues, laying-on-of-hands, casting-out-demons type. The truth in Christ is simple, yet you allow yourself to be deceived by the underhanded skills of Satan.

Thanks be to God for the restored ones like Paul who were not afraid to get a little foolish with us and give truth and sound doctrine. Baby, you had better know that's love. Sometimes correction doesn't seem fair but if you learn from it, you can obtain wisdom. Now that's the truth.

You need to know that you don't have to put up with fools gladly. There are restored ones who have walked where you are going and who have vital information for you that will give you a determination to stay in the will of God. This determination will also give you inspiration that will lead you to revelation from God. It is foolish not to listen to the restored ones, even though some of you find it more comfortable to listen to fools who want to give you their options. Instead of pointing you to the Word, they say, "Well, if I were you, I would do this or if I were you, I wouldn't do it like that."

For example, you may be trying to become debt free, but the fools will tell you, "Ain't no way in the world you'll ever become debt free." Not only are they fools but they are also dream killers. Don't share your dreams with fools. They're not going anywhere, don't want to go anywhere, and don't want you to go anywhere. They are content with being fools. And guess what; if you are content listening to them and taking their opinions as truth, you are a fool too.

The restored ones are not fools. Restored ones will give you biblical principles and truth, integrating the Word with their Godly experience.

Paul continues to sarcastically admonish the Corinthian church in II Cor. 11:16 by saying, "I repeat: Let no one take me for a fool. But if you do, then receive me just as you would a fool, so that I may do a little boasting" (NIV). He's saying that the Corinthians seemed to like to listen to fools, so if they took him to be a fool, maybe they'd listen to him too. Proverbs 14:9 makes it clear, though, what a fool really is. It states, "Fools mock at sin, but among the upright there is favor" (NKJ).

Later in the II Corinthians 11 passage, in verse 20, Paul shows his readers that they aren't as wise as think they are. He writes, "For you put up with it if one brings you into bondage, if one devours you, if one takes from you, if one exalts himself, if one strikes you on the face" (NKJ). Paul says you are the fool to allow someone else to bring you into bondage and accept it as truth. You might have been told, "You will never amount to anything, you will always be a crackhead, no one will ever love you for you, no one will marry you with all your children. You will always be like your no-good papa or mama. You will always have to stay in our fellowship." These are words of bondage. People will exalt themselves over you, physically and/or verbally degrade you, belittling your self-worth, or even call you a curse openly or under cover when you know that you are a blessing.

If you let their words be as truth to you, you're not as wise as you think you are.

Just as listening to fools causes us to suffer and keeps us from restoration, so does sin. Sin not only causes suffering and lack of restoration, but it also causes us to lose our joy. Psalm 51:11-12 says, "Do not cast me away from Your presence, and do not take Your Holy Spirit from me. Restore to me the joy of Your salvation, and uphold me by Your generous Spirit" (NKJ). In these verses, because his sins are before him, David is seeking God. He saw Bathsheba bathing and he desired her. He became intimately involved with her and she became pregnant, but she was another man's wife. Nathan, the prophet, confronted David about his doings. In other words, his sins found him out. In the midst of David's recognition of his sin, he still did not want to be cast from the presence of God nor did he want God to take the Holy Spirit from him. David cried out to God with aspiration, *Restore! Give back to me that which I lost.* David clearly said, "Restore to me...." He made it very personal. And what he wanted restored was his joy, the inner part of himself, which he had wantonly and willfully given up. David also knew exactly what he needed. He needed the salvation that only God could give him. He needed God's total work in re-establishing a right relationship between them.

Whether you listened to fools or fell into sin on your own, you must realize that God wants to renovate your mind. He wants to renew your way of transmitting and processing information. What you see is not what God sees. You see a feeble, weak, hopeless, dead situation; He sees a vibrant opportunity to restore you. He is saying, "Let Me put enough fire into your life so that the impurities (dross) will be brought to the top." That fire might manifest itself as any number of things: problems with your husband or wife, job stress, or road rage. The fire might come through children, co-workers, church members, family, homies, dawgs, girlfriends, or your boyz, those loved ones or things that are very dear to your heart. Once the fire exposes the impurities, let God deal with you so He can restore your way of thinking. He wants you revived in the mind. Those things that you pronounced dead, He may want to bring back to life.

You see that's what God did with my husband and me. In August 2002, he was in a car accident and was placed on life support. My prayer was *Lord if this man isn't going to live for You with his whole heart, remove him out of my life.* (He was almost dead anyway.)

I can almost hear some of you thinking that sure was a cold way to think, but I also know that some of you have thought those same kinds of thoughts. Come on now, tell the truth and shame the Devil. Just know that if you have, you have actually prayed witchcraft prayers in the name of Jesus.

Anyway, maybe you never saw death as a way of escape from your problem. From my point of view, that was my ticket out of the trouble, my escape route to be able to live happily ever after in the Lord, stress free. This picture appeared in my mind to be perfect. Every night that he was in the hospital, I became more and more confident that he would not be coming home. All I saw was a release from arguing, no money given to the drug dealer, and I would be paid by the insurance company. This picture looked perfect. In my mind, I had bills paid off and everything; however, God had another plan.

My husband was released from the hospital. I was so entrenched in my selfish desire to rid myself of my trouble my way, while driving him home from the hospital I actually had the nerve to ask God "Do You know what You are doing? This was my chance for freedom."

Let me tell you how God turned this dead situation around and now we are restored in the Lord, enjoying each other as never before. My husband had to decide enough was enough and wanted to walk in the newness of life. In September 2002, Evangelist Sadie Brunson ministered to me and said God was about to do a new thing in my life, but it was going to take six months to do it. At the end of 6 months, it would be well worth the pain I had to endure.

In October, my husband became incarcerated because of the drama from the accident and other past issues. The judge said he could give him 30 years; however, he was going to give him four years and suspend three years and six months. That sentence left just six months for him to serve in the county jail.

I remembered what God had just said a few weeks before. Let me tell you, it was hard for me to get enough strength to lift myself from the bench in the courtroom to walk out. I was going home alone, not knowing how the bills were going to get paid or what was going to happen from there. I made it to the car with tears in my eyes. When I started the car, my CD player began. I heard the voice of Pastor Fooks preaching a sermon entitled *No Pain, No Power.* I listened to that CD and I cried to God all the way home, realizing my marriage was going to be restored by this situation.

My husband was released in 51 days and has walked in the newness of life with a determined mind ever since. He is not going to let anything pluck him out of God's hand. He's determined to be restored with his motives being right. He has a heart for the homeless and substance abusers. He wants to make a difference in society and advance the Kingdom of God.

As of April 2003, six months after God spoke to me prophetically, we were the Pastors of Oasis Living Word Ministries in Salisbury, Maryland, under guidance of Apostle William Smack and Pastor Brendell Smack of Agape Ministries in Seaford, Deleware, along with Dr. Michael Torres from New York who is known nationally and internationally.

Yes, we have been restored and God is still not finished restoring us. We are in love and enjoying each other using our suffering to glorify God. We have taken our dry and barren seasons and allowed God to nurture us so that through Jesus Christ; we are fresh living water to others in their times of hardship.

In February 2005 my husband put a vision into reality through his faith in God. His desire was to build us a home with his own hands. He started digging the footer with $1,200 as our cash flow. Every piece of lumber, the siding, the shingles, the front step, the drywall, everything was purchased by faith. As of January 2006 the house was completed and we are giving God all the glory.

God has allowed us to be His Oasis to others by being examples of His living Word. Surrender to suffer because to live in Christ is gain. What if God had answered my prayer to let my husband die back in 2002? It's a good thing our times are in God's hands, not ours. I thank God that He didn't answer that particular prayer.

Now understand, my husband and I still face oppositions which I like to call cycles. So get ready because the cycle will began again.

Chapter 6

The Cycle Begins Again

stated in chapter five that my husband and I have been restored but God is still not finished restoring us. You need to know that for every mountaintop experience you have, there will be some valley experiences as well. When everything is going well in your life, don't get too comfortable because it is only for a season. As long as we are here on earth, cycles will begin and end. You may not experience the exact same issue that plagued you as before, but you need to know something else is going to surface, so don't let it take you by surprise.

Cycles have their way of bringing balance to your life. If the events in your life were always good, you wouldn't be able to relate to hardships. You wouldn't understand refinement, which involves being reduced to a pure state. Cycles cleanse us by the removal of bad deeds, wrong thoughts, ill-willed hearts, or immoral characteristic, through purification. The purification is the process by fire (circumstance or situations) that allows the dross to come to surface so that it can be removed until the refiner sees his reflection.

If we do not have the mind of Christ during these cycles, what has become bright in our lives–whether it is something, someone or even ourselves–may appear dull and indistinct. Lamentations 4:1a states, "How the gold has become dim! How changed the fine gold! (NKJ)" This is something to think about. What "gold" in your life has lost it luster? What used to sparkle in your eyes but is now dull? Is it your relationship with God, a spouse, other family members, your job, yourself, your home, your church, your children, your car, your dog, your cat, your boyfriend or girlfriend, or your money? Maybe you are asking yourself, *What is it?* Fine gold is something precious, valuable and dear. That which is precious, valuable, and dear will become murky if we aren't familiar with the process of cycles.

I don't care how anointed you my think you are. As quiet as it's kept, we have all struggled at one point or another with the process of cycles. Here's what happens: God tells you He is going to take you to another dimension in Him and you get all excited. Then when the process of the cycles begins, you wonder what in the world is going on! You thought great things were about to happen and then all kinds of torment break loose in your life. Guess what, that's exactly what's supposed to happen. It's all part of the process to get you to the next facet in Christ.

I remember one evening in early October 2004. I was riding to church and a line from a song popped into mind. "Where do broken hearts go?" I couldn't remember who had sung it or even if it was a gospel or secular song. Since that was the only part of the song that came to me, I had to call one of the members from church, Clea, and ask her if she remembered the song. She did remember the song and recalled that it was a Whitney Houston song. She didn't know all of the words; however, she was able to obtain the words of the song and gave them to me.

I didn't understand why this particular song came to me, but from time-to-time, I would read the words that she had found for me. Then there came a cold November day, just like in the words of the song. I went directly to the Lord and said, "So here I am and can you please tell me where broken hearts go? Can I find my way home?" I knew home was in His presence but that seemed so far away with the pain inside being so intense. I said to the Lord, "How off could the timing be for this problem to come into my life now? Lord, you know the church is about to enter into the *Gathering of the Reaper's* conference. How, in your name Jesus, can I host a conference with a pain so horrendous?

The day before the conference began, I was ready to call all the guest pastors and tell them the conference was cancelled. Nevertheless, I remembered something that God had spoken to me a few days before I experienced this cold November day. He had told me, "Don't take it personal." At the time, I didn't know it was going to seem so personal. Although I was hurting, and home in His presence felt too far away, I pressed on. The safest place to me was His open arms but at the time I didn't feel Him holding me. I knew His love was there, but I couldn't find it through the agony. I needed some help!

I emailed two ladies, Kim and Lisa, who I knew would intercede on my behalf. The email went as follows:

I am desperately requesting you two to pray for me today. I am in a very lethal low place today. The best word to describe it is a grievous feeling. There are periods of time when I break down and cry as if one were grieving. This place is new and different but extremely hard. It feels like my heart is deteriorating but yet I know new life is coming out of this. This place is very strange to me. I know I don't normally go into much detail but I feel I have to explain what is happening on the inside of me. It's like I have to get this out of me. This is a 9-1-1 call for me.

Also include in your prayers that Billy and I will come out of anything we face more anointed, more powerful, sharper in discernment, and wiser than what we have ever been before. Immovably Standing, PV.

The reason my heart was broken is that I had a crazy thought and acted on it. My husband's cell phone was on the counter charging and he wasn't at home so I decided to be nosey and listen to his voice mail messages. While listening to the messages, I had a few concerns about a couple of the messages. I didn't want to approach him aggressively because I knew I was in the wrong in the first place. At first I was going to let it go and not say anything; however, the curiosity was eating me up inside plus I was being convicted at the same time. So I confessed to him of my wrong doings a couple of days before the conference and he got upset stating that I just didn't trust him. I told him that wasn't the case and then all chaos broke out in a major argument. Everything had gone wrong. We said things we shouldn't have said to each other. It was just a mess, so much to the point that he left the house for a couple of days. Therefore, because of my negative actions, I was in a lethal low place.

During the process of cycles, you will experience lethal lows and heroic highs; just don't let either experience take you out of your character. A lethal low experience can take you out of your character causing you to become withdrawn, dysfunctional, spiritually paralyzed, moody, disturbed, annoyed, and perturbed. You will be tempted to focus on the situation instead of on Christ. Yet on the other hand, a heroic high experience can take you out of character in the other direction, causing you to be arrogant and to think more highly of yourself than you ought to. You could become high maintenance and controlling, seeing others as peons, and making yourself a god.

Throughout the process of cycles, two types of people tend to show up—celebrators and haters. It is crucially important that you discern the difference between the two. Know who is for you, the celebrators, and who is against you, the haters. If by chance you get the two confused, you could be devoured for your lack of discernment.

Take note: for every situation you will not have the same haters and celebrators. You need to know, at any given moment, that they can switch roles and you can't take that personally.

Even though the celebrators and haters exist, putting a great amount of focus on them can make you become double-minded because you are busy watching them instead of Christ. Since celebrators and haters can sometimes switch the roles that they are playing, it's difficult to remain alert to what is going on.

For example, you know someone as a celebrator and you think he is on your side, then the person flips and becomes a hater. *You wonder, how can this person do or say these things when we walk in agreement?* Check this out: that person is already double-minded by virtue of the fact that he can switch roles. That's why the person is unstable.

People like this are undercover schizophrenics who don't know their own true identity. We don't know how many personalities we are dealing with in one person. Schizophrenics can switch personalities in a matter of seconds. They can be celebrating you one second then hating you the next. They can be celebrating on this Sunday and then hating you by next Sunday. They can say they love you and your family, then wish all kinds of damnable stuff on you all. That's crazy!. But I'm going to expose this demon today. No more will you think you are crazy when God is showing you bits and pieces. You know something isn't right but you just can't put your finger on it. That's God revealing his truth to you, letting you know to be aware of the danger ahead. How many times do we ignore His warning signs trying to give people the benefit of the doubt because they are in the faith?

These "switcher" types of people have two problems. Internally, they are hindered from receiving and giving love from God and man. They hunt for attention, can't cope with chastisement and correction, and are extremely seductive. Seduction not only implies a sexual connotation, but it also means to prudently allure mentally. Externally, they capitalize on the faults of others, prevent the person from seeing himself or herself, walk in disobedience, and are openly judgmental of others.

The breeding ground for this type of personality is rejection. Somewhere in their lives, they didn't get the love they longed for. Since they didn't get that love, they have become rebellious against God and man. That's why it behooves you to know who the celebrators and haters are. Going through cycles will either make you or break you, so don't become confused. Remember cycles come to bring us balance.

In Zephaniah 3:15 the word states, "At last your troubles will be over, and you will fear disaster no more," You need to know there is an appointed time that troubles won't have you fearful due to failure, misfortune, tragedy, catastrophe or adversity. You need to understand that with His love, He will calm your fears. So don't get unbalanced because your heroic highs don't last long or they are so far and few in between or that your lethal lows seems to be without end. God wants to show us the altitude of His love. His love will allow us to forgive with realness, if we could stop concentrating on ourselves. Even through there is a cyclic rotation of change that permeates our lives it isn't about us—it is all for His glory!

During our cycles, at times we may feel embarrassed but the book of Zephaniah speaks to this. Verse 18b states, "...you will be disgraced no more." No longer do you have to feel embarrassed when rough times in a cycle come around. God knows what He is doing when he allows situations to come your way. Your haters have the repercussions of verse 19. "And I will deal severely with all who have oppressed you. I will save weak and helpless one; I will bring together those who were chased away. I will give glory and renown to my former exiles, who have been mocked and shamed." The book goes on, and in verse 20, God shows us what will happen to the haters. "They (the haters) will praise you as I restore your fortunes before their very eyes. I, the Lord have spoken" (NLT).

Now the question to you is, will you surrender to suffer so that God may get the glory out of your life? No matter what comes or who goes, will you let Him have His way in your life? God wants you to reap the benefits of your suffering to make you perfect or mature. He wants to establish you, strengthen you, and settle you in Jesus' name.

Now I speak unto you as Paul spoke in II Corinthians, 13:11, "Finally, brethren, farewell. Become complete. Be of good comfort, be of one mind, live in peace and the God of love and peace be with you." Amen.

Epilogue:
By Pastor Brendell
Smack

The author of this book, YoVanda Jenkins, conveys the process of trials to triumph. This is a book demonstrating a divine process. The meat of the book depicts suffering and great adversity at a young age. I gather from this book that this young woman was chosen to suffer so that others will not have to suffer. Many of us choose to suffer silently, especially if it is a trial that brings embarrassment to us personally or to our family. This author had things unspeakable to come up against her, in relationships, in marriage, and even in family challenges. I see that even in suffering, you can gain great strength and courage. I noticed that some cycles were repeated at times, but I believe this happened so that she could prove to her adversities that she could do all things through Christ that strengthened her.

Many are the afflictions of the righteous, but the Lord delivers them out of them all. I believe she learned this early on in her process. God made her a great example of fortitude and determination. Through this book, we should get the message that regardless of the type of tragedy we face, there is life after, and God can use our trials to make us great and victorious. I believe she became victorious. No matter how much we have to go through, there is always victory if we want it badly enough.

Thank you, Vanda, for going through your due process so we can have hope.

Printed in the United States
84502LV00002B/1-99/A